PIRATES
in the
CARIBBEAN

(THE HIGH RISKS TO SECURE FREEDOM)

PAUL NUNEZ

ISBN 979-8-88540-233-0 (paperback)
ISBN 979-8-88685-075-8 (hardcover)
ISBN 979-8-88540-234-7 (digital)

Christian Faith Publishing
832 Park Avenue
Meadville, PA 16335
www.christianfaithpublishing.com

Printed in the United States of America

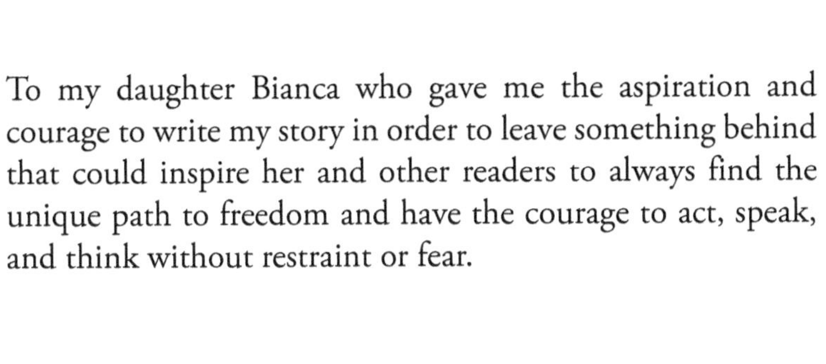

To my daughter Bianca who gave me the aspiration and courage to write my story in order to leave something behind that could inspire her and other readers to always find the unique path to freedom and have the courage to act, speak, and think without restraint or fear.

CONTENTS

INTRODUCTION

In the twenty-first century, people continue to love American culture in numerous nations throughout the world as in the past. It might be due to its advanced science, technology, music, movies, sports, or other forms of media. For example, American culture and its liberties appear to attract teens and young adults more than any other age group or country. This is notably true in Western Europe and adjacent nations of the United States.

This remarkable autobiography of Reinaldo who became a pirate in the Caribbean is about fleeing oppression and seeking freedom. The narrative, set in 1960, is similar to many others. It's about a teenage boy who wanted to be someone for himself, liked Elvis Presley, Buddy Holly, The Platters, and most other rock musicians in the '50s. He wanted to have the freedom like any other Cuban or young person to eat and dress, do and go where he wanted, enjoy rock and roll music and American movies, and embrace American culture and possibly live like one. The difference is that for Reinaldo, everything comes to a halt all at once.

Transportation in Cuba remains the same (Havana, Cuba, 1959).

American tourists frequently visited Havana's luxury hotels, beaches, and casinos. Cuba was one of Latin America's most sophisticated and successful countries.

Cubans from all walks of life were banded together to oppose corrupt dictator Fulgencio Batista, including students, merchants, businessmen and politicians. They wanted a change from years of chaotic dictatorship, so consequently, no one saw socialism would totally paralyze the island, including transportation and turning it into one of the worst dictatorships in history.

View of Havana, Cuba (1959)

Havana, Cuba's capital, was a vibrant and glitzy city. The country's economy had risen substantially in the early half of the century, fueled by the selling of sugar to the United States. Cuba ranked fifth in the hemisphere in terms of per capita income, third in terms of life expectancy, and second in terms of automobile and telephone ownership.

Reinaldo as a student (1959)

The curriculum and academic content taught in schools, similar to that in the United States, rapidly changed, and all the teachers could say was, "That's how it used to be." In 1960, many high school seniors found it impossible to complete their senior year.

CUBAN REVOLUTION

Fidel Castro deposed the dictator Fulgencio Batista in 1959. Batista had been a progressive, democratically elected president in the 1940s, but a military revolution restored Batista to power in 1952. He canceled elections, crushed dissent, and made deals with the United States Mafia to enrich himself at the expense of poor Cubans.

Reinaldo, seventeen, was in Havana when Cuba was overrun by an ostensibly democratic revolution that turned out to be anything but democratic: Fidel Castro was a communist. It was as if a terrible shadow had descended across the entire country, casting a pall over tens of thousands of youths like Reinaldo.

The curriculum and intellectual contents taught at schools similar to those in the United States were unexpectedly changed to reflect a socialistic ideology. Many professors, instructors, and teachers pretended to accept the new curriculum for fear of losing their jobs and, perhaps, labeled as "counter-revolutionaries". Others jumped at the opportunity to promote the communist doctrine as a superior alternative to capitalism.

The island had devolved into a big riot from city to city between the new government of Castro's and Batista's followers, confrontations, gunfights, arrests, and quick executions without trials for the "counter-revolutionaries."

Simultaneously, Havana was also like a "Brazilian Carnival" for those happy to see Batista go.

The revolution began with a variety of economic, political, and social systems at various stages of development. Radio stations in Havana, such as Radio Kramer, which used to broadcast the newest American rock music, were soon renamed the "Voice of the Revolution!" Reinaldo's favorite music had evolved into a fusion of doo-wop harmonies combined with Cuban Conga and tribal rhythms, which he recognized well enough to understand the lyrics. There was nothing wrong with the genre since Cuban comparsas had existed for decades, but rock and roll's demise in Cuba was due to political considerations.

Because the previous dictatorship was friendly to the United States, the Cuban socialist regime rejected everything about it. Gambling and rock and roll have a negative influence on young people, urging them to embrace the "old Cuban sound" and turning boys and girls into ardent nationalists.

A young woman incorporated into Fidel
Castro's liberation army (Havana Cuba)

The young socialist revolution developed a youth crowd, which is one of the aspects explaining how and why the Cuban Revolution has survived to this day.

A policeman is targeting looters of a casino with his gun.

Confrontations, gunfights, arrests, and fast killings without trial for the "counter-revolutionaries" erupted across the island as a large riot spread from city to city between Castro's new government and Batista's supporters.

A triumphant entry for Fidel Castro in Havana, 1959

Having ousted General Fulgencio Batista's American-backed tyranny, Castro's arrival in Havana represented a decisive triumph for his 26th of July Movement, as well as the start of Castro's decades-long dictatorship over the island nation.

Reinaldo, as one in the crowd, felt the same enthusiasm that millions felt. But it didn't last long.

Castro's policies included socialist reforms and priorities that were hostile to foreign corporations, resulting in a rivalry with the United States and a close partnership with the Soviet Union.

Reinaldo as a revolution supporter (1960)

In the 1960s, youth began to play an increasingly crucial role. Youth culture and politics were on the rise around the world at the time, but Reinaldo was skeptical of the unique circumstances he faced without the United States.

Havana (1961)
Armada soldiers use force to discourage opponents of Socialism

Only two years after one tyrant is overthrown, another one takes over and begins to suppress its opponents. According to Fidel Castro, "Opposing socialism is the same as support 'Counterrevolutionaries.'" Conviction meant imprisonment or death.

SO WHY A REVOLUTION?

Cuba had many of the same qualities as the United States, including in terms of automobiles, fashion, and the majority of household goods. Havana was a sparkling and energetic city that had grown in size and activity like any other bustling American metropolis. In Havana, you might find Florsheim shoes, Sears, Woolworths, and department shops selling well-known sportswear brands like McGregor and the latest trends as well as luxury European designs by Christian Dior, Givenchy, and Yves Saint Laurent, among others.

Cuba had kept up with the times, ranking second in per capita vehicle and telephone ownership and first in the number of television sets per capita. Because of the United States, Cuba was the most advanced country in the Western Hemisphere, making capitalism a viable economic system.

Because it further intensified the American capitalistic system, Hollywood-based motion picture productions were no longer in cinemas. Someone made the culture change. Instead, Chinese-made combat films extolling "triumphant" socialism, extensive Russian propaganda, and condemnation of the United States, as well as assistance from the media and the press, dominated the airwaves almost immediately.

A FADING CULTURE

Reinaldo and those like him would have no choice but to adapt or bear the consequences. To find whatever "made in the USA" was available from the previous dictatorship, he would go to the waterfront where Americans used to venture, clubs, and local bars. El Paseo del Prado or the Malecon would have jukeboxes still playing the 45 rpm singles of the rock and roll revolution. Albums up until the early 1960s were becoming increasingly scarce by the day. By 1962, they were all gone.

The district of nightclubs, on Paseo del
Prado, at night (Havana 1959)

Havana Cinema featuring American films (1959)

American films began to vanish quickly in the first year of the new communist revolution. Nothing American would be allowed to "invade" the minds of the people, especially the youth. "Revolution! Revolution! Revolution!" is all people would hear. They established a cinematographic department within the Ejército Rebelde's Dirección de Cultura (Rebel Army's Culture Division), which funded the production of communist propaganda documentaries, Chinese- and Russian-made films emphasizing military might; virtually unknown protagonists to the public were replacing well-known American dramatic artists. Film is "the most potent and provocative form of artistic expression, as well as the most direct and widespread vehicle for educating and presenting ideas to the public," according to this new system. This was upsetting and depressing for teenagers who were accustomed to American entertainment, music, and film.

Retail Stores and Empty Shelves

China imports were becoming more evident, but you couldn't buy more than one pair of shoes per year under Cuba's Ration System, which had already been implemented. "From light to darkness" was the finest way to describe this era of transition.

The country was undergoing a significant cultural transformation. The peso (the Cuban currency at the time) was replaced with a new currency, depicting the *heroes* of the revolution: Fidel, Camilo, and other socialist *heroes* of the revolution. Churches were closed, and Christmas celebrations were prohibited, along with the peso. With Russia as his principal ally, Castro found himself at the center of a perilous fight for political supremacy.

Many of Reinaldo's age believed that escaping Cuba at any cost was the best way to dodge the draft and avoid being transferred to Russia for further brainwashing. The prospect of being brainwashed was unappealing to individuals who were born after WWII (1945) and had experienced a democratic government system. Reinaldo's generation admired and sympathized with the United States Constitution because it guaranteed individual liberty.

The New Cuban Peso

A dying city
With rations in place, most hotels and
casinos looked like museums

Early in the new decade, as the newly founded Cuban Revolution veered toward a Marxist-Leninist political system, relations with the United States grew cold, and the middle-class lifestyle of Cubans had evaporated.

The national Cuban currency changed surprisingly overnight. Fidel Castro had been secretly working on creating a Marxist Socialist system with close ties to the Soviet Union, rendering the old currency worthless. This was clearly a dictatorial move. The old currency must be exchanged for new currency at government-controlled banks. A cap was set so the upper-middle class could only get a fraction of their substance. As a result, everyone became equally poor—instantly.

From the *New York Times* (Friday, August 18, 1961),

> The nation's currency was being changed. During the next two days, Cubans must hand over their old pesos—all of them. In exchange, they would get a maximum of 200 new-style pesos in cash, with the rest "credited" to their names in a government-controlled "bank account," from which from then on they might draw 1,000 pesos after a week and no more than 100 pesos per month. All old pesos were declared worthless.

Cuban Prime Minister Fidel Castro and Soviet
Premier Nikita Khrushchev (1960)

Victorious Fidel Castro, with Russia as his main supporter, felt he could spread socialism into Latin America. He developed a rigorous interactive relationship with Nicaragua's Sandinista National Liberation Front (FSLF) in the early 1960s. Then he proceeded to export socialism to Venezuela and other countries.

Central Park in Havana.
Displaying a wreath of solidarity for Russia's Communism

Fidel Castro expresses support for a socialist government system that is not autonomous as the one before. Ironically, this demonstration takes place in front of the marble statue of José Marti, who died in war defending Cuba's independence.

THE EXODUS

By 1961, a major exodus of Cubans had begun to abandon the island in whatever manner they could, as Fidel Castro's new government had aligned itself with Russia and China, as well as the rest of the socialist countries, in order to exert vigorous and aggressive social control over the island.

"The land of the free and the home of the brave" was a favorite slogan of Cubans in general. Reinaldo had just one more dream: to be able to live in the society he fantasized about. In fact, his buddies said he was getting close to looking like one of his rock idols. His favorite female was Martha since she looked like an American girl, blond with green eyes, which he preferred over blue eyes, although he had told his buddies before "she looked the part."

SUPPORT FOR THE REVOLUTION

Reinaldo pretended to be a member of the *armadas* during the beginning of the revolution. Though he never fought in a battle, it was simple for him to join as a revolutionary figure in any arm-training center and obtain instruction. Since the majority of the population advocated backing the revolution, without doubt, all you needed was an olive-colored uniform and a pistol. He donned the green suit and set off to explore the island.

Revolution supporters obtained firearms confiscated from Batista's army and police, including an M1A1.45-caliber Thompson submachine gun with a thirty-round magazine. Reinaldo was initially terrified, but he kept his feelings to himself. He had no desire to fight because what he was seeing was too rigorous, inflexible, and not democratic.

Reinaldo had a job with "The Imperial Eagle," an ex-Canadian insurance agency where he had to take a bus, but the vehicle would frequently stall on the streets due to a lack of parts.

Time passed slowly, and nearly every basic commodity manufactured in the United States was quickly vanishing from the island. The government had seized all private businesses and was continuing to consolidate all American-owned businesses. It was no longer a virtue to be a private owner.

All Cubans were required to listen to Fidel
Castro's speeches on Marxism-Leninism

In support of his Marxist worldview, Fidel Castro gave
a speech that was equally lengthy and sophisticated on live
radio and television at a studio in Havana. It would require
two hours to respond to just one inquiry. Not a typical states-
man's traditional, diplomatic utterance but a persuasive declaration of his political ideals.

FADING SUPPORT

By this time, the revolution had become a god. Any intentions to leave Cuba lawfully, whether on a tourist visa, a student visa, a medical visa, or to visit a family member in the United States, was prohibited unless you were granted a special visa by a religious organization, blood relative, be over the age of fifty, and with the right connections in Cuba. People must stay in support of the revolution.

The crackdown was legalized and enforced by security forces, state-linked civilian sympathizers, and an inept judiciary. Many were imprisoned in deplorable conditions throughout the island, thousands more were harassed and intimidated, and entire generations were denied basic political liberties.

Such abusive actions created a toxic climate of fear in Cuba, obstructing the enjoyment of basic fundamental rights and pressuring Cubans to demonstrate their allegiance to the revolution. Showing support for the contrary is simply a "counter-revolutionary" act punishable by law to this day.

Reinaldo refused to join parties or celebrations since he was being harassed for not openly supporting the revolution. One soldier became inebriated and pulled his gun on Reinaldo, intending to kill him; but thanks to the efforts of others, he was subdued, and Reinaldo was able to flee the celebration.

Cuba achieved progress in health and education; however, much of this progress was hampered by prolonged economic hardship and repressive policies. Pharmacies, which previously provided a plentiful supply of first aid and life-saving medications, had all but vanished by 1962. Inner-party members, on the other hand, would keep any medical aid from the United States to themselves.

Early in the revolution, there were a lot of meetings and talks, but Reinaldo, who loved America, found them unsatisfying

This new government, according to Reinaldo, "was much crueler than the previous one." But the revolution needed time to usher in a new order that would benefit the entire Cuban populace rather than just a small corrupt clique. Unfortunately, it never occurred.

The Cold War between the United States and Russia was felt in Cuba on a grand scale. For weeks and months, the lights on the entire island were out, placing fear in the hearts of people, telling them that the United States would be bombing the cities; Cuban forces were mobilized everywhere, and Russian Mig-17 and Mig-19 fighter jets were continually flying. Any plausible strategy to flee Cuba was put on hold due to the upheaval. The fact was, the revolution needed public support.

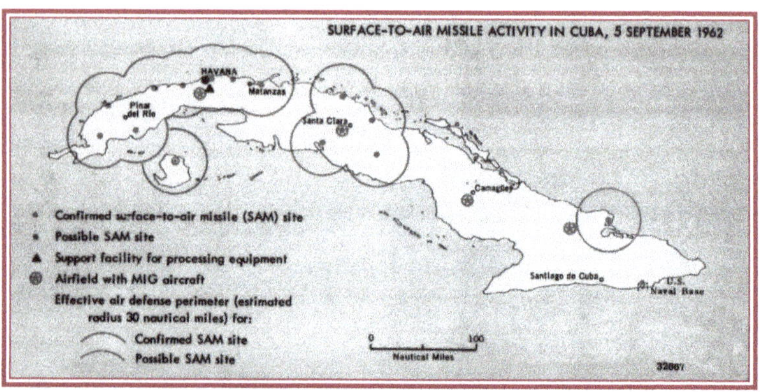

(Wikipedia free encyclopedia)
Map created by American intelligence
showing Surface-to-Air missile activity in Cuba (1962)

The US believed the Soviet Union was constructing missile facilities in Cuba as early as August 1962. During that month, its intelligence services received data on report of MIG fighter jet sightings from observes on the ground.

Life in Cuba had become even more stressful after hearing news from Miami, Florida, radio that U-2 spy planes discovered surface-to-Air missile sites at eight separate locations. The future grew dreadfully grimmer for nonsocialist adolescents who had little regard for Castro's ostensibly "noble" goals.

HOPE TO MAKE CUBA A REPUBLIC AGAIN

The invasion of Cuban exiles from Miami on April 17, 1961, was a dismal failure, with one thousand four hundred Cuban exiles from Miami, launching a bungled assault at the Bay of Pigs on Cuba's south coast.

According to the plan, the invasion would be supported by the Cuban people and elements of the Cuban military. The United States had given up hope of seeing Cuba become independent by destabilizing Castro's socialist rule and installing a noncommunist administration that would be friendly to the free world. Reinaldo's aspirations were only short-lived; instead, the failed invasion bolstered Castro's administration, which went on to openly declare its determination to embrace socialism and pursue stronger links with the Soviet Union. It also prompted the Kennedy administration to reconsider its Cuba policy.

In retaliation for the finding of Soviet missile sites on the island, President John F. Kennedy declared a *quarantine* on Cuba. He declared the United States to have a comprehensive embargo on Cuba, which is still in effect today. Most Cubans understood the embargo, but the revolution was using it to demand more sacrifice out of poverty-stricken people.

A SHIP FROM AMERICA

In compensation for the survivors of the one thousand four hundred Cuban expatriate POWs in the Bay of Pigs, the embargo delivered a United States ship to Havana Harbor with tractors, food, and pharmaceutical supplies. It was obvious that Cuba's economy was already in bad shape.

The ship had docked within three hundred yards from the ferry boat route, which runs between Old and East Havana on a regular basis to the city of Regla. Reinaldo and friends contemplated buying ferry tickets, with the intention to hold up the ferry and compel the captain to get near the American ship and to get on board. It would have failed miserably.

Reinaldo and four friends had conducted a *trial run* (at night) and discovered that the region was tightly encircled by army soldiers who were on the lookout for any suspicious activity. Any effort to board the ship would have resulted in a swift and deadly shooting. The project was quickly scrapped.

Poverty indicators were evident everywhere as the
shortage of essential resources grew worse

Well-known for its wealth of sugarcane, variety of
tobacco products, and world-famous cigars, the government
started to limit sales of the majority of domestic goods to its
own citizens.

As a result of the widespread shortages of almost all
foods and consumer goods, Cuba's economy deteriorated
to a degree worse than those of some third-world countries,
Eastern Europe, and the Soviet Union.

Havana's Port

After the failure of the invasion at the Bay of Pigs, a US ship sends fifty-three million dollars in food and medical supplies provided by firms across the US as a condition for the release of over 1,100 Cuban POWs. Many onlooker nationals breathed a sense of liberty when they saw the ship, but Castro used the invasion to further solidify his power.

A PLAUSIBLE ESCAPE STRATEGY EMERGES

Havana to Key West, Florida, only ninety miles away is the shortest distance between Florida's Key West island and Cuba's capital, Havana. If they must leave by boat for the purpose of sea navigation, the water distance across the Strait of Florida in nautical miles would be approximately 103 miles.

Unfortunately, that was the most traveled, as well as the most closely monitored by Cuban air surveillance planes. Hundreds have previously tried and failed with several being murdered in the process by Cuban soldiers.

The survivors' horror stories had two effects: They scared people to death, and they helped Castro's dictatorship keep a tight grip on "would-be deserters." It will make the rest of the uncommitted think twice before attempting to flee Cuba's north coast: "A suicidal expedition" was the catchphrase for any who wanted to try.

Reinaldo would seldom see or chat with his parents, relatives, acquaintances, or even Martha. He needed to find a *strategy* or medium to take a course of action and formulate the modus operandi. The yearning was so strong in his mind he couldn't get the thought of *leaving Cuba* out of his mind.

Instantaneously, the Cuban government, headed by the
Communist Party of Cuba, tightened its grip over the media

There was strict control of all media circulation and particularly foreign periodicals to hotels frequented by tourists. News, information, and comments were also monitored and controlled. The boundaries of laws prohibiting propaganda against the government were strictly enforced against all journalists. The government owned every major media outlet, prohibiting any private ownership of broadcast media.

Cuba's South Coast

The Caribbean Sea filled with nothing but water

The island's south coast, as well as the Caribbean Sea's Isla de la Juventud and numerous tiny archipelagos south of the island, was practically unaffected by air monitoring. The south shore had an undiscovered peacefulness; nonetheless, there were amazing fishing activities, and where there are fishermen, there are boats!

However, because Cuba is located where the northern Caribbean Sea meets the Gulf of Mexico and the Atlantic Ocean, the trek would take at least two hundred strait miles south, two hundred miles southwest, and six hundred miles northwest via the Gulf of Mexico's center. With God's help, they should be able to reach Brownsville, Texas, which was the nearest port in the United States from that direction. That would necessitate superb planning as well as a miracle!

Any boat capable of making such a journey, if any existed, would belong to Cuba's fishing procurement distribution department, which was established in 1960 as part of the Cuban government's nationalization program, which involved taking control of all private companies, real estate, farmland, and other income-generating assets such as boats, planes, trucks, and agricultural equipment. Taking a boat by force would be deemed "buccaneering piracy." Anyone caught would be executed right away on counter-revolutionary charges: Any revolution militia had the license to kill on that basis.

With no visual air reconnaissance by Cuban authorities, the Caribbean Sea wide open, with only Isla de la Juventud and other small archipelagos south of the island, the journey was long but appeared safe. Furthermore, the modest south beach from which to flee exuded a pleasant quietness. The plan's approval was aided by the small number of fishermen and three larger boats to choose from.

TOP SECRET

The aim was to create a plan and figure out how to get started without being caught. Reinaldo had an uncle who worked for the postal service in a small town forty-five kilometers south of Havana, and another twenty kilometers south was a fishing community that relied on fishing for a living. The families were content with a beach that was primarily mud, and with a boardwalk for swimmers, it was perfect. However, the community had a military post with a few soldiers on duty, and this would represent a problem for any would-be pirates wanting to take a boat by force.

The purpose was to see if anyone in the village was receiving United States mail. If so, that would mean they have family members in the United States. Would he want to join them? If "Yes," he had most likely considered a scheme or two at some point in the past to flee. It was like fishing to locate the correct individual but was worth investigating!

The Investigation

Reinaldo's uncle didn't know any or didn't want to provide any information, concerning his postal service obligation, but he did offer a few names of people who had relatives in the United States. And as he put it, "Everybody knows who has families in America. They're all fishermen!"

It seemed reasonable, after all, that in a tiny town, everyone knows everybody, and what harm could there be in asking a few questions? Who would think a conspiracy to flee the island in a small boat from this beach could be suspected?

Who in their right mind would consider any plot to flee from the south coast? The answers were positively, "No one!" Because any boat big enough was owned by the government, therefore manned by members of the communist regime.

Searching for men of courage with a will for liberty was risky. They must carefully examine their political views and philosophy; if they know somebody who knows somebody, they then take time to find if they can be trusted. After many months of search and secret communications, trust began to build up among new friends who had a similar way of thinking. Fleeing Cuba was the only way to find freedom and liberty, and who didn't want that? All had this settled conviction that a good plan had to be the common denominator for it to work. First, they will formulate a course of action and provide drawings of the geographical area with a contingency plan and discuss it.

STRICT DISCIPLINE

No real names will be disclosed due to the nature of the plan and to avoid reprisal by the Cuban authorities against their families. Just their position, office, and role in which they knew each other. It may take courage and discipline to do this, but it was worth the effort. Each man must then self-discipline himself to adopt rigid behavior.

Safety Precautions

Even though no one was hurt or wounded in this scheme, a ship from the Cuban government was taken, which constituted a significant source of income for the syndicate and their families, and they would regard this as an act of *piracy* since Cuba has some of the Caribbean's most well-preserved marine ecosystems, and any form of aggression to it would be fatal.

It is now December 1963. There were no obvious flaws in the plan. Reinaldo and three other companions went to the beach as *beachgoers* to familiarize themselves with the region and particularly its physical features. They knew it was the lowest elevation point of the Caribbean Sea at sea level, and the terrain is primarily flat with some rolling plains and without hills.

At the time, there were three huge boats, ranging in length from fifty-two to sixty feet, docked beside the river that went into the sea, and a number of small motorboats too small for authorities to suspect any escape voyage. Some of the small boats belonged to local fishermen, while others belonged to out-of-town residents who come in the summer season. Reinaldo and his friends were all there to have a good look since there was no fishing activity in December.

The river (a water channel) ran parallel to the only road that goes into town for about two miles. The military facility was located exactly at the end of the road, roughly three yards from the water. Any considerable size boat docking or large party arriving at the beach would be considered *unusual*, immediately drawing the attention of the soldiers.

They had decided that taking off in any of the larger boats from the beach was just too dangerous and wouldn't stand a chance.

Capturing the boat when at sea is the only way to get away. It won't be easy, but it may work. To add to the challenge, for approximately four kilometers before reaching the beach, there was nothing but marshes, brier bush, water channels, and sinkholes on both sides of the road. To evade the residents and guards, the crew would have to go through the unused-uninhabited wilderness that was rough and difficult to trek; but it also provided a natural barrier to give them a sense of protection and security.

They had discovered that when the fishing season was open, all of the larger boats would spend days at sea, and finding them in the wide ocean would be somewhat problematic; nevertheless, fishermen knew where to fish, so they were counting on Samuel's skills, which became very helpful later.

The Chosen Ship

The ship was *La Valiente Del Mar* (*Seaworthy*). She was fifty-two feet long. *Not bad!* thought Reinaldo, and by now they were about sixteen of them. By the time the plan was developed and put into operation, for whatever reason, there were a total of twenty-two men. They couldn't dispute at this stage of the game because the extra bodies were quite helpful in getting all the pieces of the plan together.

The Team

Members of the Cuban Revolutionary Armed Forces (Spanish: *Fuerzas Armadas Revolucionarias* [FAR])

They began with few members and subsequently expanded to a few more. The military has always been Cuba's most powerful institution. There were four members of the militia, the military force that is raised from the civil population to supplement a regular army in an emergency and four fishermen (the shipmates), as well as the captain of the boat *Seaworthy* and Samuel, who owned a small fishing boat Victoria, and his friends.

THE ALTERNATIVES

Samuel would have to go *fishing* in his boat throughout the day and return to shore in the evening, but not to the settlement. He planned to remain three miles west of town, away from all the buildings and army posts. Then sit and wait for the team to arrive from their swamp adventure. The team will arrive in a private taxi from the city; they will be picked up one by one, including some from a small town forty-five kilometers south of Havana; and then they will continue on the deserted road to the beach until they could reach the river—which was essentially a water spring that flows parallel to the road like a river and into the sea.

The guys will be dropped off, and then they would go through the marsh, brier, thorns, and other obstacles to reach the coast in the moonlight—meet Samuel and his boat, hopefully. He'd be sending them a sign that the coast is literally clear, get aboard, and head to the sea in search of *Seaworthy* with the fishermen from our contact list.

The term *seaworthy* fit her name very well. She had an ancient bus diesel engine from the 1950s, as well as a fifty-gallon drum full of extra fuel, sails, and fishing gear. No one questioned her age or the state of her condition by looking toward the bow. Both the port side and starboard were faded and worn out. Who wants to come out as a negative thinker by pointing out any probable problem at this point?

A crew of armed soldiers, outfitted with military equipment on board, and a sizable boat immediately begin heading to the Caribbean Sea seemed like a very solid plan to fail, everyone thought.

"So let's proceed with the strategy because it appears to be a sound—foolproof strategy and feasible." That was a unanimous agreement.

Water channel adjacent to the road

The team would have to cross the water channel that leads to the beach and walk through the thicket in order to come out far enough from the beach.

Communication among team members will remain confined to a one-on-one basis from this point forward. Reinaldo would communicate with only one team member: ideally, a close friend, to appear normal discussion among friends.

In the months ahead, the guys were cautious in their preparations, making sure everything was in order. Finally, by June, they would have a departure date. Everyone must maintain a low profile. If anyone gets detained or questioned by authorities, it will set off a chain reaction in which many will be killed. So far, ten of these sixteen men, if caught, would be sentenced to death and executed immediately.

PLOT IN ACTION

The team was ready by night. On the evening of June 21, each man was designated to a specific location. By midnight, the trustworthy gypsy cab driver was riding from Havana to the final drop-off site before the beach. He was passing through several towns. In the last small town, he had a pickup, then continued south another twenty kilometers where he would drop the human cargo then turn around for home.

The driver earned more money that night when they gave him all the cash they had on hand—Cuban currency was useless anyhow, and he deserved it.

Then came the march through the marshy ground, with the moon on their backs. During the march, no one spoke a word. They were hiking without a trail for the first for over an hour at the mercy of thorns and swamps. "The shore!" whispered someone. Samuel was there with the extra guys onboard Victory he brought with him. The total number of men is now twenty-two, counting the men on *Seaworthy*.

The Unexpected Happened

While still on the beach, the first unanticipated misfortune became a challenge: Victory's motor won't start. Getting the boat started was a crucial moment. It was taking too many pulls to respond; something more serious was evident. It was a mechanical failure the team could not afford to get caught in broad daylight, and they were running out of time. One discovered a choke knob on the boat's floor. "That was it," they declared. The motor finally started, and the first signs of dawn appeared on the horizon. It was totally an unexpected stumbling block, but now they were on the way. Fortunately, there was fog, which helped them avoid being spotted, but it also made it difficult to locate *Seaworthy*, which they would have had to locate out at sea.

Second Complication

There was a second unforeseen obstacle that occurred after almost one hour of sailing in the fog. They ran aground on an archipelago, and the boat got stuck in the sand. Samuel's boat Victory was extra heavy with so many on board; the *passengers* began to disembark.

When a second *roadblock* appeared to be real, Marti, the group's most spiritual member, proposed a prayer. "Let us all pray," he said. It was the appropriate thing to do as one observer put it: "A boat that gets trapped in the middle of the ocean needs prayer!" The truth was that they couldn't afford to have the hull damaged and the boat be taken on water. Someone like God could help them out. Everyone got out of the boat with lifted spirits and started pushing until they were well out into deeper water again.

The Wrong Boat (Third Unforeseen Obstacle)

The men came upon a boat that looked pretty much like *Seaworthy*. They had navigated six to seven nautical miles out to sea. Because there was still some fog in the area, and Samuel couldn't see far enough to tell what's what, they mistakenly approached the wrong boat. The boat belonged to a different fishing company unfamiliar to the team. They were caught!

Confused

They had no idea what was going on at first, but because most of the men looked like Revolutionary Armed Forces, they assumed they were conducting some sort of routine inspection. They instantly realized the men were deserters fleeing the island and begged to leave them behind on the promise that they wouldn't say anything when they returned to land.

Samuel asked, "*La Valiente Del Mar?*"

"Ahead, another five hundred yards."

They had to make an urgent decision.

Tense Moment

They all agreed that they couldn't trust them. "They'll have to come along with us until we get *Seaworthy*," they announced.

"You can't do this," they cried. "We have our families and jobs and are not interested in coming along!" Was their response.

"You're going with us until we're on our boat, then you can go back."

As the team stood on the roof of Victory, and the rest were charging their guns, it was obvious the message was clear: "If you don't follow orders, someone is going to get hurt." There was silence for a few seconds. They were persuaded by the sound of charging firearms, the panic, and the danger involved. They led the team to *Seaworthy*. Victory and the men followed.

Seaworthy was in front of them since the sun had burned away much of the fog. Their connections onboard *Seaworthy* with the shipmates had the engine started for the escape as soon as they arrived. "Wait, I'm coming too!" screamed one of the captive boat's fishermen. So he got on board as well, bringing the total number of guys on board to twenty-three.

Victory was virtually torn into two by a hail of bullets, and she sank like a stone. There was an anguished look on Samuel's face, but Victory was no longer needed, and "there is no going back." For safety concerns, the captain of *Seaworthy* was unaware of the plot at the time of the hijacking, but the team knew he had a daughter in the United States, and he was readily convinced.

(graphic or sketched situation suggested)

What are the options for the detainees? It was unanimously determined that they would take them along for at least a day with their boat after which they might return to Cuba the next day. They handed a rope to their skipper to "tie to bow" so *Seaworthy* could tow them at full speed. No one knew how far south they'd gone, but they figured that after a full day of sailing (twenty-four hours) at maximum speed, and another full day for them to reach the Cuban beach, they'd be able to convince authorities that "forty-eight hours of navigation should be enough." That was the case.

However, it is not yet safe: The next day, around mid-morning, additional boats in the distance seemed to be more fishing businesses, maybe from *Isla de la Juventud*. Then aircraft (two) started flying about in the sky. All uniformed personnel must remain in the cabin and wait for the four shipmates to drop their nets and begin fishing. The planes vanished. Maybe the Cuban pilots weren't expecting piracy in the Caribbean Sea. Or was real fishing the ideal decoy? Or were the pilots just allies of the counter-revolutionaries since they made no meaningful effort? Whatever it was, it worked; and that afternoon, they ate raw lobsters.

THE PERFECT STORM

After three days of sailing toward the Gulf of Mexico, the sky became the darkest it had ever been. It was around 10:00 p.m. *Seaworthy* being battered by a violent storm with very strong winds and rain, the ship was wooden; and according to the old skipper, she was built in Spain in the 1920s, with very little maintenance due to shortage of supplies and materials that had long been vanished from hardware and general stores everywhere. All she could do was short fishing trips, not from sea to shore.

She was taking a lot of water as the men and the crew hurriedly grabbed whatever they could find to draw water while trying to hold on because of the violent winds. In its most basic form, old-fashion hand bailing to remove water that had entered a ship was nonstop. The perfect storm was now the *fourth* unanticipated complication that brought the faith of the men to almost a complete halt. Each man grew more and more despondent. It was extremely difficult to get all of the water out. Loading a few containers of water and dumping them into one of the deepest parts of the sea was literally a drop in the bucket. "It'd be impossible to save her," they reasoned among themselves, and all hope of survival had vanished.

By the dawning of a new day, the winds and rain had stopped, but *Seaworthy* was sinking: The ship was clearly not deserving of her name.

The White Dot on the Horizon

The storm was gone, but not without leaving its marks. Seaworthy could no longer move as quickly as before. They were all looking out for some hope when around 10:00 a.m. everyone noticed a white *dot* on the horizon that was increasingly getting bigger and bigger. It was a freighter traveling across the Caribbean Sea on its way north. The skipper had learned about a "Cuban vessel" that had left Cuba's south coast through radio and had come to offer assistance. They too had been through the storm, but cargo ships are, by design, genuinely seaworthy. Upon knowing the sinking condition with no food and water, the captain decided to take them on board. "We're heading north to the United States," they explained, and there was the joyous loudest yell from the rescued team.

After the captain had consented, ropes, straps, and hooks were quickly lowered to load *Seaworthy* on the freighter's deck, and the skilled shipmen were transferring *Seaworthy*, team, and all with the ship's crane as they would a container. *Seaworthy* looked more like a paper boat once on deck.

Cruising through the Gulf

The trip north seemed like a luxury cruise line: wonderful pleasant crew, retelling stories, and pure delight celebrating their rescue. On the fourth day of sailing, land appeared. It was America's shore.

The team had gathered on the deck to enjoy the view of the American coastline. It was a beautiful day in the morning, the ideal moment to see the new world. The ship was going slowly through the seventeen-mile ship canal of Port of

Brownsville, Texas. The team could hear dock workers' voices coming across the water.

The recovered guns by ship's officials had remained on the ship's deck during the journey, and the majority of them, especially the Czechoslovak CZ Model 25 machine guns, had rusted away during the few days' journey. *Seaworthy* became the property of the shipping company that rescued the pirates in the Caribbean.

Port of Brownsville

For Reinaldo, the sight of the Port of Brownsville, at the southernmost tip of Texas, was the glorious sight of freedom.

LIBERTY AT LAST

As they approached the cargo dock, setting foot on United States soil was the highlight moment for the team. It was a joyful and loud shout, "FREE!" They were greeted by a jubilant gathering: members of the press, enthusiasts, and, of course, immigration service officials. For security reasons, interrogation had to come first; but eventually, they were awarded permanent status in the United States. When everything was documented, and they were free to talk to the press, the one repeated statement from the team was, "There is no price too high one can pay for freedom."

Once he stepped foot on the ground, he would be free of oppression, tyranny, and dictatorship, as well as the storm and his concerns. The seventeen-mile-long ship channel seemed now to be as long as the journey itself. They remembered their prayers—how God had brought them safe and sound to free land.

The New York Times

23 Cuban Refugees Landed In Texas by Rescuing Ship

BROWNSVILLE, Tex., June 27 (AP)— Twenty—three Cubans arrived here today and told of capturing a fishing boat, nearly starving and being rescued at sea.

The 23 were picked up by the Colombian freighter Ciudad Bucaramanga Barranquilla last Wednesday. The refugees, all men, had exhausted their food supply and were eating raw lobsters.

Immigration authorities took the men to headquarters for questioning. A ship's officer said the refugees told him they boarded and captured the fishing boat last Sunday.

MAKING A HOME
IN AMERICA

The new "residents" were well received by various religious institutions that made it possible for each to relocate wherever they had friends or relatives. Most of them had friends and relatives in Florida; others were being picked by close relatives.

Reinaldo made it to Florida where he was reunited with friends he had in Cuba. Later, he decided to go to California where he had closer friends. Having a desire to advance, California was difficult for him because of an abundance of the labor force at the time, so he moved to New Jersey to find better work, better pay, and to go to school perhaps at night.

Five years later (1969), Reinaldo met a young girl who won his heart. They got married in 1973 and moved back to California. They have a married daughter and a married granddaughter with a great-grandson. They remain in Texas close to each other. Reinaldo's wife is an American girl with blue eyes, just as he dreamed of at seventeen.

Both are Born-Again Christians who love Jesus Christ, and Reinaldo thanks his Lord every day for the liberty he's been able to enjoy in the United States.

ABOUT THE AUTHOR

Paul Nunez was raised in Cuba as a Catholic. Despite the fact that he was unfamiliar with the religion's doctrine, he had a deep impression that God was real and at some place. Paul was pretty well out of faith-based teachings after Fidel Castro's revolution. The revolution was making it even more difficult for people to receive a true concept of God's nature since the revolution was an atheistic movement that discouraged all religious activities and teachings.

As a result, any understanding of the Bible or God remained unspoiled and undeveloped. He was taken aback by the cultural shift. Being unable to be who he desired was painful, and life became more difficult by the day.

However, his knowledge of the United States, as well as what he had studied in school, movies, magazines, and tourist sites, had piqued his interest sufficient to desire and be part of it.

First and foremost, as stated in the Declaration of Independence, "We hold these truths to be self-evident, that all men are created equal, that they are endowed by their Creator with certain unalienable Rights, among them are Life, Liberty, and the pursuit of Happiness." Cuba had lost any possibility of coming close to the goal.

The idea of fleeing the country was his sole option for allowing liberty to reign in his heart. But "true liberty", as Paul puts it, came when he met Jesus Christ personally. That, in his view, is why *Pirates in the Caribbean* was worth the danger.